An Arms Control Strategy for the New Europe

Lynn E. Davis, Project Director

Project Team: Christoph Bertram, Ivo Daalder, Richard Darilek, Ian Davidson, Hilmar Linnenkamp, John Roper, Michael Wills

Supported by The Ford Foundation

RAND

PREFACE

This report concludes the activities of the RAND Project on Arms Control, which has been funded under a grant from The Ford Foundation. The project began in 1990, when a team of security analysts and journalists from the United States and Europe won The Ford Foundation's competition for grants on the future of arms control. Our goal has been to design arms control measures appropriate for the evolving security structures in Europe and to introduce our ideas and analysis into the public debate on the future role of arms control.

The Project on Arms Control produced an assessment of the Treaty on Conventional Forces in Europe, by Ivo H. Daalder, soon after its signing in 1991. We have provided commentary on various arms control issues through newspaper articles and journalistic pieces. In the spring of 1992, we defined a strategy for arms control in the new Europe, which we presented to the delegations to the Review Conference of the Conference on Security and Cooperation in Europe (CSCE) in Helsinki and circulated to government officials in the various CSCE capitals.

We would like to thank The Ford Foundation for its support of this project. The institutional setting for the project shifted from the Johns Hopkins Foreign Policy Institute to RAND. Our thanks to both for their support.

Director, Project on Arms Control

Lynn E. Davis, Vice President, Army Research Division, RAND

Project Members

Christoph Bertram, Diplomatic Correspondent, *Die Zeit*, Hamburg

Ivo Daalder, Director of Research, Center for International and Security Studies at the University of Maryland

Richard Darilek, Senior Researcher, RAND

Ian Davidson, Correspondent, *Financial Times*, London

Hilmar Linnenkamp, German Armed Forces Command, General Staff College, Hamburg

John Roper, Director, Institute for Security Studies, Western Europe Union, Paris

Michael Wills, Independent TV Producer, Juniper, London.

SUMMARY

One current but deeply mistaken assumption is that arms control in Europe has become, in effect, a relic of the Cold War. Although that historic East-West conflict ended favorably, both for Europe and for arms control, future peace and security in Europe are still not guaranteed. Since Europe remains one of the most heavily armed regions in the world, any serious deterioration of its security situation could have catastrophic consequences.

Arms control can help combat such dangers. It has a continuing role to play in addressing Europe's new insecurities and instabilities. It can even help move Europe toward a new political-military order based on cooperative security policies, the net result of which could be removal of military force as a factor in relations among states and creation of a genuine community of interests. This paper argues, therefore, that arms control should not be held hostage to the return of peace or the establishment of a collective security framework in Europe, but instead should be pursued ambitiously for its own potential contribution to peace and security.

The arms control record to date provides a firm and impressive foundation upon which to build an ambitious agenda for the future:

- The nuclear powers have announced their intention to eliminate virtually all their tactical nuclear forces.

- The U.S.-Russian agreement will reduce their strategic nuclear arsenals by an historic 70 percent over ten years.

The number of major conventional weapon systems deployed in Europe will be reduced by some 40 percent to a level 125,000 pieces below what was deployed in 1989. The maximum level of military personnel will be that declared by signatories of the Treaty on Conventional Armed Forces in Europe (CFE). A panoply of regulations now govern conventional military activities in Europe, thereby increasing transparency, ensuring observation and inspection, and establishing constraints for such activities.

What is missing, however, is an overall strategy for future arms control in Europe, with objectives appropriate to the new security situation. Such a strategy would involve pursuing arms control on four fronts simultaneously, to

- Help build confidence among the newly independent states and contribute to peace-building efforts

- Confirm by treaty the positive developments in military forces and activities under way in Europe

- Manage the demilitarization of interstate relations in Europe and, over time, foster a community of interest throughout Europe such that disputes are resolved peacefully

- Reduce significantly the role of nuclear weapons and strengthen the global nuclear nonproliferation regime.

The strategy itself seeks to replace old concepts and ways of thinking about arms control by setting goals and suggesting measures tailored to the new security challenges facing Europe.

In conclusion, this report contends that peace should not be left to chance. The potential remains for conflict in Europe; as long as there are armaments, security will have a military dimension. Arms control, therefore, should be expected to play a key role in ensuring Europe's future security.

CONTENTS

TABLES

Chapter One

THE NEW CASE FOR ARMS CONTROL

Now that the Iron Curtain has come down, and the military confrontation between East and West has ended, many assume that arms control has lost its utility for contributing to security in Europe and has become, for all practical purposes, a relic of the Cold War. This assumption is deeply mistaken.

Arms control made a valuable contribution to the security of Europe during the Cold War, most notably in enshrining the notion of negotiated balances in the nuclear arsenals of the two superpowers. This contribution reached its apogee during the late 1980s and early 1990s, as the Cold War was drawing to an end. Significant reductions have been achieved in nuclear and conventional weapons. Nuclear weapons in the republics of the former Soviet Union are being brought under Russian central control. Military forces and their activities throughout Europe have been opened to observation and inspection. Measures have been negotiated to promote greater confidence and security. But future peace and security in Europe are still not guaranteed.

The end of the Cold War means the end of one kind of insecurity in Europe. But other kinds of insecurity and instability loom. Europe will need to develop new security policies and structures appropriate to these challenges. For both, arms control will have a vital and central role to play.

It is true that the simplest model of arms control, in which the arsenals of two opposing powers or alliances are counted and balanced against each other, as a way of containing and limiting their confrontation, is no longer easily applicable to post–Cold War Europe.

There is no military confrontation between East and West to cause fears of attack; the Warsaw Pact has been dissolved; and the Soviet Union itself has disintegrated into its component republics. The previous calculus of a potential balance, therefore, no longer exists.

But even with the military confrontation behind us, the end of the Cold War has not automatically brought with it a new era of peace and serenity. On the contrary, the whole of Eastern Europe and the republics of the former Soviet Union are going through traumatic transformations of their societies, their economies, and their political systems. The consequences are bound to be unpredictable and may be destabilizing for the continent as a whole. In the former Yugoslavia and some of the republics of the former Soviet Union, the first terrible manifestations of interethnic and regional violence have appeared. There is every reason to believe that the pattern of violence could spread. Since Europe remains one of the most heavily armed regions in the world, any further deterioration of the security situation could have catastrophic consequences.

The way for Europe to contain these dangers is to employ arms control to help move in the direction of cooperative security policies and a new European order. Through further reductions in nuclear and conventional forces, arms control can bring military capabilities into line with current political realities. Thus, arms control could help remove lingering sources of distrust and provide a hedge against a reversal of current policies among the newly independent states as they confront mounting economic problems.

Arms control offers the possibility of confirming by treaty the positive developments in military forces and activities under way in Europe and of helping achieve a significant reduction of remaining armed forces in European societies. Arms control can also aid in removing the dangers of nuclear weapons in Europe and, thus, strengthen the global nuclear nonproliferation regime. Moreover, arms control can help build confidence among the newly independent states in Europe, by regulating armaments and introducing confidence and security-building measures. Experience, particularly the Israeli-Egypt case, also suggests that the settlement of conflicts is best assured if arms control is an integral part of the settlement process. Demilitarized zones, cantonment and demobilization of combatants, bans on offensive weaponry, and verification by third parties could contribute to peace-building efforts among the warring ethnic and religious groups in Europe. In these ways, arms control can directly address the security challenges that are emerging in the wake of the Cold War.

But arms control also has a positive role to play in the transition from the old to a new European order. It can help create a community of interests throughout Europe wherein military forces are removed as a factor in the relations among states. It can contribute to forming expectations that conflicts will be resolved peacefully, through a curtailing of the most provocative offensive forces, an emphasis on collective rather than the unilateral employment of military forces, and increased transparency in military activities and deployments.

Arms control need not be held hostage to the return of peace in Europe or to the establishment of a collective security framework. Americans and Europeans have demonstrated that sufficient political cooperation and will exists for negotiating significant arms control agreements. The arms control record to date provides a firm and impressive foundation upon which to build an ambitious arms control agenda for the future.

This report has two main parts. It begins with a description of what arms control has accomplished since the end of the Cold War. It concludes with the elements of an overall arms control strategy, which seeks to reduce the dangers still lurking in Europe's security landscape and, for the longer term, to promote a new European security order.

Chapter Two

THE ARMS CONTROL RECORD

The end of the Cold War produced radical reductions in nuclear and conventional weapons. The nuclear powers have announced their intention to eliminate virtually all their tactical nuclear forces. The United States and Russia have agreed to reduce their strategic nuclear arsenals by 70 percent over ten years. Both countries have suspended nuclear testing, as has France.

The number of major conventional weapon systems deployed in Europe will be reduced by some 40 percent to a level 125,000 pieces below that deployed in 1989. More significantly, the Treaty on Conventional Armed Forces in Europe (CFE), which was predicated on the existence of two opposing military blocs, has been adapted to conform both to the collapse of the Warsaw Pact and to the dissolution of the Soviet Union itself. Conventional military activities, first regulated by the 1986 Stockholm Accord, have been subjected to further observation and constraints. The transparency of all military activities in Europe has been enhanced by the combination of additional confidence- and security-building measures (CSBMs) agreed to in the 1990 and 1992 Vienna Documents and the inspection and observation regimes contained in the agreements covering nuclear and conventional forces. The ability of any one country in Europe secretly to prepare for military operations against other states has been all but eliminated.

NUCLEAR WEAPON REDUCTIONS

Driven by fears of a loss of control over Soviet nuclear weapons following the failed Moscow coup of August 1991, and the subsequent disintegration of Soviet central political authority, the Bush Administration moved to create new incentives for the elimination of the potentially most dangerous of these weapons, nonstrategic nuclear forces. These weapons were deployed in many of the former Soviet republics, making it difficult to ensure their control and safety. In September 1991, President Bush announced a major unilateral change in U.S. nuclear policy, including the elimination of all ground-launched tactical nuclear weapons and the removal from surface ships and submarines of all nonstrategic naval weapons, in the expectation that the Soviet Union would reciprocate. President Mikhail Gorbachev obliged with the promise of unilateral reductions in air, land, and sea tactical nuclear weapons.[1] (See Table 1.) Russian President Boris Yeltsin in January 1992 confirmed the reductions in the nuclear forces of the former Soviet Union.[2] The other European nuclear powers, France and Great Britain, followed with their own significant changes in nuclear deployments.[3]

These various initiatives have led to the consolidation of all Soviet tactical nuclear weapons on Russian territory. With the exception of some 600 to 800 tactical nuclear bombs, U.S. nuclear weapons have been redeployed to U.S. territory. Apart from their strategic ballistic missile–carrying submarines, the Russian, British, and American navies have been shorn of nuclear weapons under normal peacetime circumstances. The United States and Russia will destroy about half of their tactical naval nuclear stockpile, storing the remainder at central locations. Great Britain will eliminate all its tactical naval

---

[1] See "Remarks by President Bush on Reducing US and Soviet Nuclear Weapons," *The New York Times*, 28 September 1991; "Gorbachev's Remarks on Nuclear Arms Cuts," *The New York Times*, 6 October 1991.

[2] "Russia's Policy in the Field of Arms Limitation and Reduction," Statement by Russian President Boris Yeltsin, 27 January 1992, reprinted in United Nations, General Assembly, A/47/79, 29 January 1992.

[3] France has announced the removal of nuclear bombs aboard its Jaguar tactical aircraft, the elimination of its Pluton short-range missiles, and the cancellation of the Hades missile. The UK has eliminated its ground-based launchers, removed tactical warheads from its ships and cut its air-delivered weapons in half. See Charles Miller, "UK Announces Nuclear Reductions," *Press Association*, 28 September 1991, *FBIS-WEU*, 30 September 1991; "Mitterand Addresses News Conference," *FBIS-WEU*, 12 September 1991; "Hades Missile Scrapped," *Jane's Defence Weekly*, 20 June 1992, p. 1041; and "Letter to the Secretary-General of the Conference of Disarmament by the Leader of the United Kingdom Delegation," United Nations, *CD/1156*, 23 June 1992.

Table 1

Tactical Nuclear Weapon Reductions

United States	Russia
Deployment	
• Withdraw all 1,700 land-based weapons from Europe and South Korea and all 500 sea-based weapons "usually at sea" from surface ships and attack submarines.	• Withdraw all tactical nuclear weapons from non-Russian Republics by 1 July 1992. • Withdraw all naval weapons from surface ships, "multipurpose" submarines, and land-based naval aircraft.
Land-Based Weapons	
• Dismantle all 1,300 artillery shells and 850 short-range missile warheads.	• Dismantle all 6,130 artillery shells, short-range missiles, and nuclear mines; remove all 3,000 warheads for air-defense missiles from deployment areas and dismantle half.
Sea-Based Weapons	
• Eliminate all 1,100 nuclear depth bombs aboard ships and land-based naval aircraft; place nuclear sea-launched cruise missiles (SLCMs) and tactical bombs in secure storage.	• Eliminate one-third of all 3,075 weapons and place remainder in secure storage. Halt production of SLCMs. • *Propose,* on a reciprocal basis, the elimination of all naval tactical nuclear weapons, including SLCMs.
Air-Based Weapons	
• Remove all weapons from South Korea; cut those in Europe by 50 percent to about 600–800 weapons. • Halt development of the short-range attack missile–tactical (SRAM-T) to fill the tactical air-to-surface missile role.	• Eliminate half of all 3,100 bombs and missile warheads. • *Propose,* on a reciprocal basis, to remove from combat units of the frontline tactical air force all nuclear bombs and missiles and place in central storage.

SOURCE: Ivo H. Daalder, *Cooperative Arms Control: A New Agenda for the Post–Cold War Era*, CISSM Papers 1 (College Park, MD: Center for International and Security Studies at the University of Maryland, 1992), p. 26.

nuclear weapons. Virtually all U.S., Russian, British, and French ground-based tactical nuclear weapons will be eliminated, including all tactical nuclear missiles, artillery shells, and land mines. The exception will be Russian nuclear warheads for air-defense missiles, only 50 percent of which will be destroyed.

As a result of these initiatives, less than 7,000 tactical nuclear weapons will remain of the nearly 25,000 deployed around the world in the mid-1980s. Most of those remaining will be stored rather than deployed with active forces. Over two-thirds of these were deployed in Europe. Of these, some 5,000 weapons are Russian air-defense warheads, tactical nuclear bombs, and naval weapons. The United States will retain some 700 tactical nuclear bombs, most of which are deployed in Europe, and 1,000 sea-launched cruise missiles and bombs for carrier-based naval aircraft, which will be stored in the United States. France and Great Britain will also retain small inventories of substrategic air-delivered nuclear weapons.

In July 1991, the United States and the Soviet Union completed nine years of negotiations on the Strategic Arms Reduction Treaty (START), which reduced their strategic offensive nuclear arsenals by about a third, to 7,000 to 9,000 weapons on each side.[4] The breakup of the former Soviet Union initially complicated implementation of the treaty and held up its ratification for some months.

Strategic nuclear forces are located on the territories of four newly independent states: Byelarus, Kazakhstan, Ukraine, and Russia. The goal was to ensure that all of the nuclear weapons and facilities of the former Soviet Union were covered by START and that only Russia of these newly independent states would be a nuclear-weapon state in the future. A new protocol to the treaty was negotiated under which all four republics were together identified as the U.S. treaty partner, and the three non-Russian republics pledged to sign the nuclear Non-Proliferation Treaty (NPT) as nonnuclear weapon states "as soon as possible." Kazakhstan, the United States, and Russia have ratified START, and Byelarus is expected to do so shortly. The Ukrainian government is committed to ratification, but parliamentary opposition is delaying approval. Both the U.S. Senate and the Russian parliament have insisted that the treaty can only enter into force once all parties to the Lisbon protocol, including Ukraine, have ratified it.

---

[4]For a summary and analysis of START, see "Strategic Arms Reduction Treaty: Analysis, Summary Text," *Arms Control Today*, Vol. 21, No. 9, 1991.

The protocol not only opened the way for START ratification and implementation but also laid the basis for more far-reaching reductions in those U.S. and Russian strategic weapons that would remain following full implementation of START. During the Washington summit meeting between Presidents Bush and Yeltsin in June 1992, a joint understanding was reached that would further reduce U.S. and Russian weapons. They signed the START II in early 1993, mandating reductions in U.S. and Russian forces in two phases: In phase one, to be completed by the year 2000, each side's forces must be reduced to 3,800 to 4,250 (thus modifying the START I ceilings); in phase two, forces would be reduced to 3,000 to 3,500 on each side. (See Table 2.)

Table 2

U.S. and Russian Strategic Forces: 1990–2003

	Pre-START (1990)		Current (1992)		START II Phase 1		START II Phase 2	
	U.S.	CIS	U.S.	CIS	U.S.	Russia	U.S.	Russia
ICBMs								
Launchers	1,000	1,398	930[a]	1,015[b]	530	697	500	609
Warheads	2,450	6,612	2,370	6,115	800	1,489	500	609
SLBMs								
Launchers	648	940	480	832	432	424	432	264
Warheads	5,568	2,809	3,840	2,696	2,016	1,840	1,728	1,730
BOMBERS								
Launchers	276	162	232[c]	100[c]	120	57	104	57
Weapons	4,436	1,506	3,908	1,266	1,432	912	1,272	912
Warhead Total	12,454	10,927	10,118	10,077	4,248	4,241	3,500	3,251

SOURCE: Estimates based on "Factfile: Past and Projected Strategic Nuclear Forces," *Arms Control Today*, Vol. 22, No. 6, 1992, p. 36; *Treaty on the Reduction and Limitation of Strategic Offensive Forces*, Memorandum of Understanding (Washington: ACDA 1991); and U.S. Department of Defense, "Fact Sheet on U.S. Strategic Nuclear Forces" (Washington: DoD, 19 June 1992); Ivo H. Daalder, *Cooperative Arms Control: A New Agenda for the Post-Cold War Era*, CISSM Papers 1 (College Park, MD: Center for International and Security Studies at the University of Maryland, 1992).

[a]370 Minuteman II missiles are off alert.

[b]90 SS-19 missiles in Ukraine and all SS-18 missiles targeted at the United States are believed to be off alert.

[c]All bombers are off alert.

In addition, the two countries will eliminate all missiles with multiple warheads based on land, limit warheads on submarine-launched ballistic missiles to 50 percent of the total, and count bomber weapons according to the actual number deployed rather than the number attributed to them, as is the case in START I.[5]

Steps have also been taken in the area of nuclear testing. In his response to President Bush's September 1991 initiative on nonstrategic nuclear forces, President Gorbachev announced a one-year moratorium on all Soviet nuclear tests in the hope "that this example will be followed by the other nuclear powers, and in this way a road will be opened up for earliest and complete cessation of all nuclear tests." President Yeltsin, in his January 1992 statement on disarmament issues, reaffirmed this commitment. In a surprise move, the prime minister of France, Pierre Beregovoy, announced in April 1992 that France would suspend nuclear testing for the remainder of the year. The U.S. Congress was next to act, when in October 1992 it voted in favor of a nine-month testing moratorium, to be followed by a limit of five new weapon tests for three years. These could be undertaken only for safety and reliability purposes. Thereafter, the United States would no longer conduct any nuclear tests, so long as all the other nuclear powers refrained as well. President Bush signed this into law, and so U.S. testing has been suspended until mid-1993.

CONVENTIONAL FORCES

In November 1990, the CFE Treaty was signed by the 22 members of NATO and the former Warsaw Pact. The treaty mandated the removal from Europe of 125,000 battle tanks, armored combat vehicles (ACVs), artillery, combat aircraft, and combat helicopters deployed within the region of the Atlantic to the Urals (ATTU). A system of zonal limitations ensured that the concentration of weapons deployed in the center of Europe would be given priority in the reductions. Agreement to a sufficiency rule, under which no one country could possess more than about one-third of the total number of weapons deployed within the ATTU, effectively capped Soviet conventional military forces below that of the combined deployments of

---

[5]For the text of the START II treaty, see *Arms Control Today*, Vol. 23, No. 1, 1993.

the NATO countries. Although the treaty as a whole fell short of its purpose to eliminate the ability to conduct large-scale conventional operations in Europe, it nevertheless represented a major step and set the stage for further reductions in conventional armaments.[6]

Ratification and full implementation of the CFE Treaty were initially held up by the remarkable changes in Europe occurring during and after the treaty's negotiation. As originally conceived, the agreement was framed as a treaty between two opposing military alliances, NATO and the Warsaw Pact, and set *de jure* alliance-wide ceilings. But it actually placed *de facto* limits on holdings of conventional military equipment of individual nations that, when combined for all members of an alliance, could not exceed half the forces deployed within the ATTU as a whole. As a result of negotiations among the six members of the Warsaw Pact, a separate treaty was agreed upon in early November 1990 that declared each country's maximum level of holdings under the CFE Treaty to be the *de facto* level of holdings. In effect, then, this separate treaty converted the alliance-wide ceilings into national ceilings for the Warsaw Pact member states.

The CFE Treaty's ratification was also delayed as a result of the Soviet Union's insistence when signing that the treaty-limited equipment (TLE) deployed within naval infantry, shore defense, and strategic rocket forces be exempt from the treaty limits. This dispute arose because the treaty limited only ground and air forces, not naval forces, and specifically exempted land-based naval aircraft from its limits. The Soviet interpretation was challenged by the other treaty signatories. In the end, Moscow conceded the point and agreed to count all TLE deployed within the ATTU as part of its declared holdings. A dispute over the removal of some 60,000 Soviet TLE east of the Ural mountains prior to the treaty's signing was also resolved when Moscow declared in a politically binding statement that it would destroy a significant portion of this equipment and deploy the

---

[6]For an analysis of the CFE Treaty, see Ivo H. Daalder, *The CFE Treaty: An Overview and an Assessment*, Project on Arms Control (Washington, D.C.: Johns Hopkins Foreign Policy Institute, 1991).

remainder in storage sites that could be readily monitored by overhead surveillance.[7]

By far the most serious challenge to the CFE Treaty came from the dissolution of the Soviet Union in December 1991. Legally complicated questions arose as to how to ensure adherence to the treaty by the eight newly independent states within the ATTU region.[8] Some of the zonal limits had the effect of dividing certain countries into more than one zone. Furthermore, disputes among the new states held up agreement on how to divide the declared Soviet maximum level of holdings among eight independent countries. In the end, an agreement was reached during a meeting of the Commonwealth of Independent States (CIS) in May 1992. This opened the way for an Extraordinary Conference of states who were parties to the CFE Treaty in June 1992 to amend the treaty.[9] (See Table 3.) The treaty formally entered into force on November 9, 1992, following its ratification by Byelarus and Armenia. Legal implementation of the treaty's provisions commenced on July 17, 1992, following agreement to this effect among the now 29 parties during the Conference on Security and Cooperation in Europe (CSCE) summit meeting in Helsinki. Full implementation of the reductions must be completed by November 14, 1995.

With the adaptation of the CFE Treaty to the new political realities completed and its entry into force now assured, the next task will be to ensure its implementation over the next three years. Differences among the former Soviet republics regarding who is responsible for destroying the excess equipment, as well as the cost of any destruction, are likely to occur in the months and years ahead. This under-

---

[7]The Soviet statements are reprinted in U.S. Congress, Senate, *The CFE Treaty*, Hearings before the Subcommittee on European Affairs of the Committee on Foreign Relations, 102nd Congress, 1st Session, March–July 1991, pp. 363–368.

[8]The three Baltic states, which gained their independence in September 1991 and who do not themselves possess any TLE, are not signatories to the CFE Treaty, although all Soviet (non-Russian) TLE deployed on their territory is subject to limitation. See "Statement of the Chairman of the Joint Consultative Group, October 18, 1991," reprinted in U.S. Congress, Senate, *The CFE Treaty*, Washington, D.C.: U.S. Government Printing Office, pp. 364–365.

[9]See "Final Documentation of the Extraordinary Conference of the States Parties to the Treaty on Conventional Armed Forces in Europe," Oslo, Norway, June 1992.

Table 3

Maximum Level of TLE Holdings in the ATTU

	Tanks	ACVs	Artillery	Aircraft	Helicopters
Belgium	334	1,099	320	232	46
Canada	77	277	38	90	13
Denmark	353	316	553	106	12
France	1,306	3,820	1,292	800	352
Germany	4,166	3,446	2,705	900	306
Greece	1,735	2,534	1,878	650	18
Iceland	0	0	0	0	0
Italy	1,348	3,339	1,955	650	142
Luxembourg	0	0	0	0	0
Netherlands	743	1,080	607	230	69
Norway	170	225	527	100	0
Portugal	300	430	450	160	26
Spain	794	1,588	1,310	310	71
Turkey	2,795	3,120	3,523	750	43
United Kingdom	1,015	3,176	636	900	384
United States	4,006	5,372	2,492	784	518
Total NATO	19,142	29,822	18,286	6,662	2,000
Bulgaria	1,475	2,000	1,750	235	67
Czechoslovakia	1,435	2,050	1,150	345	75
Hungary	835	1,700	840	180	108
Poland	1,730	2,150	1,610	460	130
Romania	1,375	2,100	1,475	430	120
Total E. Europe	6,850	10,000	6,825	1,650	500
Armenia	220	220	285	100	50
Azerbaijan	220	220	285	100	50
Byelarus	1,800	2,600	1,615	260	80
Georgia	220	220	285	100	50
Kazakhstan	0	0	0	0	0
Moldova	210	210	250	50	50
Russia	6,400	11,480	6,415	3,450	890
Ukraine	4,080	5,050	4,040	1,090	330
Total CIS	13,150	20,000	13,175	5,150	1,500

SOURCE: "Conventional Forces in Europe After CFE" (Washington, D.C.: Arms Control Association, July 1992).

NOTE: Only a small portion of Kazakh territory is located within the ATTU, and no forces covered by the CFE agreement are to be stationed there.

scores a need for the Western countries to be both actively engaged and willing to extend financial assistance and technical expertise to ensure the timely and full implementation of the CFE Treaty. Nevertheless, the conclusion of the treaty did enable the 29 parties to fulfill their earlier pledge to supplement the treaty with limits on manpower in a CFE-1A agreement. This politically binding agreement limits air and ground force personnel for each country to a level declared by each country in June 1992. (See Table 4.)

Table 4

Maximum Level of Personnel Within the ATTU

Armenia	NA
Azerbaijan	NA
Byelarus	100,000
Belgium	70,000
Bulgaria	104,000
Canada	10,660
Czech and Slovak Federal Republic	140,000
Denmark	39,000
France	325,000
Georgia	NA
Germany	345,000
Greece	100,000
Iceland	0
Italy	315,000
Kazakhstan	0
Luxembourg	900
Moldova	NA
Netherlands	80,000
Norway	32,000
Poland	234,000
Portugal	75,000
Romania	230,248
Russia	1,450,000
Spain	300,000
Turkey	530,000
Ukraine	450,000
United Kingdom	260,000
United States	250,000

SOURCE: *Concluding Act of the Negotiation on Personnel Strength of Conventional Armed Forces in Europe*, July 1992, Section II, para. 1.

NOTES: Only a small portion of Kazakh territory is located within the ATTU, and no forces covered by the CFE agreement are to be stationed there.

NA = not available. No declarations were made at the time of the agreement's signing.

REGULATING MILITARY ACTIVITIES

Under the CSCE Final Act in 1975, the member states agreed to notify the other member states of military exercises on a voluntary basis. The Stockholm Conference on Disarmament in Europe (CDE) took the next step in 1986, when the members agreed to a number of CSBMs involving the advance notification of certain types of military exercises, constraints on large scale exercises, and the observation and inspection of certain military activities.

Under the 1992 Vienna Document, the CSCE states took further steps. Military activities involving 9,000 troops or 250 tanks must be announced in advance. Such activities will be subject to observation if they exceed 13,000 troops or 300 tanks. No country may conduct military activities involving more than 40,000 troops or 900 tanks more than once every two years. Such activities must be announced more than one year in advance. In addition, no state can conduct activities involving more than 13,000 troops or 300 tanks but less than 40,000 troops and 900 tanks more than six times a year, and of these no more than three activities may involve more than 25,000 troops or 400 tanks.

The CSCE members have agreed to an annual exchange of military data on the location, strength, and composition of ground and air force units and formation. Some of these are subject to on-site inspection, either under the Vienna Document or the CFE Treaty. Military budgets must also be exchanged annually.

The transparency of military deployments and capabilities is supplemented by intrusive on-site inspections. For Russia alone, baseline inspections to check the accuracy of the data exchanged under the Intermediate Nuclear Forces (INF) Treaty involved visits to 90 facilities by American inspectors, all within 120 days. Over 100 baseline inspections have been conducted on Russian soil during the 90 days following the CFE Treaty's entry into force. The United States will conduct 68 baseline inspections of strategic nuclear facilities in the four Republics once START is ratified. In addition, all three treaties contain provisions for suspect-site or challenge inspections, including annually, for Russia, up to 20 inspections of declared facilities under the INF Treaty, nearly 20 inspections of any suspect site under the CFE Treaty, and up to 15 inspections of declared sites under START.   Given reciprocal obligations for all other signatories, it is clear that secrecy will soon disappear from the military forces and operations of all the European countries, as well as of American military forces in Europe.   In addition, under the Open Skies Treaty, each signatory state will be subject to periodic flights over its entire territory. (See Table 5.)

Table 5

Overflights Scheduled Under the Open Skies Treaty

Country	Flight Quota	Flights Received Year 1	Flights Made Year 1
Benelux	6	2	2
Bulgaria	4	3	3
Canada	12	2	4.5
CSFR	4	3	2
Denmark	6	2	2
France	12	3	4
Georgia	NA	NA	NA
Germany	12	5	4
Greece	4	3	2
Iceland	4	0	0
Italy	12	3	3.5
Norway	7	2	3
Poland	6	5	3
Portugal	2	0	0
Romania	6	4	4
Russia/Byelarus	42	28	26
Spain	4	0	1
Turkey	12	5	4.5
Ukraine	12	9	6
United Kingdom/ Ireland	12	3	4
United States	42	4	8.5

SOURCE: *Treaty on Open Skies*, Annex A, Sections 1 and 2.
NOTES: NA = not available.   No declarations were made at the time of the agreement's signing.
Flight quota refers to the maximum number of flights each party is obliged to accept annually.
Flights Received in Year 1 is no greater than 75 percent of a country's flight quota for the first year following the treaty's entry into force and is based on the number of requests of flights over its territory by other states.   In some cases, countries plan to combine inspection flights, thus accounting for the allocation of one-half flights.
Flights Made in Year 1 refers to the number of flights each party has declared it will make during the first year after the treaty's entry into force.

Chapter Three

AN ARMS CONTROL STRATEGY FOR THE NEW EUROPE

The European arms control record is now a substantial one. Arms control weathered the storm of revolutionary political change. With those changes came the opportunity for agreements significantly reducing nuclear and conventional forces. Such agreements are now in place. They can help to reduce the uncertainties that follow from the passage of ex-Soviet republics to stability. They can help make this process more controllable. In a real sense, quantitative arms control can build confidence and security.

There are many possibilities for arms control in the future, and these have been analyzed in detail by both governments and policy analysts.[1] One problem with most of these possibilities is that they seem to be addressed to a post–Cold War world in Europe that is different from the one that has emerged. The former East-West military rivalry really has disappeared—completely. Now the dominant security issue appears to be how to cope with present and future

---

[1]See the various proposals presented by governments to the Helsinki CSCE Review Conference, March 1992; James Macintosh, "Future CSBM Options: Post-Helsinki Arms Control Negotiations," in Heather Chestnutt·and Steven Mataija, eds., *Towards Helsinki 1992: Arms Control and the Verification Process* (Toronto: Center for International and Strategic Studies, 1991); Jonathan Dean and Randall Watson Forsberg, "CFE and Beyond: The Future of Conventional Arms Control," *International Security*, Vol. 17, No. 1, 1992; Jenonne Walker, "New Thinking About Conventional Arms Control," *Survival*, Vol. 33, No. 1, 1991, pp. 53–65; Jack Mendelsohn, "Dismantling the Arsenals," *The Brookings Review*, Spring 1992, pp. 34–39; Johan Jorgen Holst, "Arms Control in the Nineties: A European Perspective," *Daedalus*, Vol. 120, No. 1, 1991, pp. 84–85; Paul B. Stares and John D. Steinbruner, "Cooperative Security in the New Europe," in Paul Stares, ed., *The New Germany and the New Europe* (Washington, D.C.: Brookings Institution, 1992).

Yugoslavias. Such conflicts seem likely to characterize the future security situation in the new Europe, with the use of force remaining highly relevant to, and potentially the ultimate arbiter of, the course of events. In principle, arms control should prove equally relevant to this new security situation. In practice, however, it is unclear which arms control measures should be applied to the situation, or how they might be applied.

Another problem at present is the absence of any overall strategy for arms control in Europe, with objectives appropriate to the new security situation. What is missing is an action-oriented overview of the extent to which arms control can play a role in Europe's future security, the areas in which it can play that role most effectively, and the purposes for which it should be employed—to include peace-keeping and peacemaking, as well as constraining force levels. What follows are the elements of such an overarching strategy, one that is pertinent to Europe's current and future security environment. In the classic manner of all strategies, which attempt constructively to relate means to ends and to indicate how to proceed from here to there, this strategy dictates that arms control be pursued on four fronts simultaneously, to

- **Help build confidence among the newly independent states and contribute to peace-building efforts**

- **Confirm by treaty the positive developments in military forces and activities under way in Europe**

- **Manage the demilitarization of interstate relations in Europe and, over time, foster a community of interest throughout Europe such that disputes are resolved peacefully**

- **Reduce significantly the role of nuclear weapons and strengthen the global nuclear nonproliferation regime.**

This overall strategy for arms control in Europe seeks to replace old concepts and ways of thinking about arms control by setting goals tailored to the security challenges still facing Europe. Individual arms control measures are grouped below in ways to contribute to these goals. The purpose of such grouping is to help win support for the overall goals from political leaders and, thus, gain the attention arms control deserves from governments. Placing specific arms control measures within the context of an overall strategy should also make it easier to counter the resistance to individual measures that often arises from government bureaucracies whenever any limits are suggested for military forces or their operations.

Some of the individual measures proposed below will involve formal agreements; others may result from mutual example. Some arrangements will be wide-ranging in scope, while others could be differentiated to deal with specific problems. A variety of bilateral and multilateral fora might be used to establish new measures. Some fora already exist, and others may need to be created. Regional arrangements must be tailored to the particular situation, but the CSCE as a whole could provide an umbrella to lend additional authority.

- **Arms control should seek to build confidence among the newly independent states in Europe and contribute to peace-building.**

Among the newly emerging states in Europe, arms control measures can help reduce tensions and mutual perceptions of the threat, thereby providing the basis for the mediation and resolution of potential conflicts. In addition to exercising the rights of observation and inspection of military exercises previously agreed upon, CSBMs could be negotiated to permit nations to fly over each other's border areas. Constraints could be placed both on the size and frequency of military exercises and on a variety of other activities necessary to mobilize for war. Military operations in border areas could be constrained by setting low thresholds for activities conducted in these areas. Specific types of equipment and exercises might even be banned. Within regions, the military forces of individual countries might be reduced, perhaps based on principles of parity or equal ceilings.

In 1989, Hungary proposed a "zone of confidence" with Italy, Yugoslavia, and Austria, whereby each country would withdraw its offensive military forces from their common frontiers. The zone would contain only border guards and exclusively defensive troops and equipment. Greece put forward a similar proposal in 1991 involving the border regions of Greece, Bulgaria, and Turkey. Neither of these proposals was accepted. There was not a sufficient basis for cooperation even to establish measures to help create a stable political relationship. But the situation in the region may be changing, as violence threatens to engulf the Balkans. Turkey and Bulgaria concluded an agreement in late 1991 to constrain activities in their border areas. Romania and Hungary have agreed to a limited bilateral "open skies" arrangement for monitoring their military activities. CSCE observers are in Kosovo, in the former Yugoslavia, to help deter a spread of violence. EC and American observers are on the borders of the former Yugoslavia, ostensibly monitoring the UN economic sanctions, but also seeking to deter an expansion of the conflict.

Military deployments have been temporarily limited in the eastern part of Germany. Poland might well have an interest in creating similar zones on a permanent basis along its borders with Germany, Byelarus, and Ukraine. The Nordic and Baltic countries are discussing arrangements for reducing military forces and activities along their international borders. Limitations on military deployments and operations in border areas could also be useful among the former Soviet republics.

When conflicts arise, as among the warring ethnic and religious groups in the former Yugoslavia and USSR, measures other than arms control need to be given priority: mediation, conflict resolution processes, sanctions, and military peacekeeping and peacemaking operations. Arms control inspectors might need to be turned rapidly into crisis managers and conflict observers, able to translate aggregate ceilings into ceilings applicable to a specific region. But even in these cases, more traditional arms control should not be forgotten, for it may have a small role, e.g., in gaining agreement among the parties to regulate their armaments. This has been the goal of efforts to bring the heavy weapons and aircraft held by the Serb militia in Bosnia under UN supervision. Operational arms control can also play a role, as in the case of the no-fly zone established by the United Nations in Bosnia.

More important, arms control has a critical role to play in future peace settlements. As suggested by the experiences in Cambodia, Central America, the Middle East (notably in the Sinai and on the Golan Heights), and even in Croatia, peace-building efforts depend for their success on the successful regulation of armaments, through demilitarized zones, mutual or third-party inspections, and the cantonment and disarmament of belligerent forces.

- **Arms control should confirm by treaty the positive developments in military forces and activities under way in Europe.**

The CSCE members agreed during their Helsinki summit in July 1992 to establish a new CSCE Forum for Security Cooperation. They provided an agenda, calling for the harmonization of arms control obligations, an enhancement of CSBMs, a global exchange of military information, cooperation on nonproliferation, and a series of dialogues on force planning, defense conversion, and military contacts. The problem is that, to obtain consensus, the specification of the agenda had to remain vague. It lacks any specific commitments to further arms control measures. Indeed, the CSCE members could only agree that future levels of armed forces should be the "minimum commensurate with common or individual legitimate security needs within Europe and beyond" and "may" entail reductions, limitations, and measures of a regional character. Arms control, if left to the CSCE agenda, seems destined to lag political and military developments currently under way in Europe.

Transparency of military preparations and activities has become an accepted part of European relations. What arms control provides is a means of formalizing that transparency. The data exchanges mandated by the 1992 Vienna Document and the CFE Treaty should be extended to include logistical force components, such as the location of ammunition stockpiles and the means of transporting troops and equipment over long distances. Building on the precedent of the Open Skies Treaty, Russia and the United States should include all their territories under the information and monitoring provisions of these agreements. Observers should be permitted to inspect a broad range of military forces and activities, not only the equipment limited by the CFE Treaty. Joint centers should be set up and given the task of examining and interpreting the data on military forces that will be exchanged annually under the various treaties.

The detailed exchange of annual defense budgets should also cover procurement plans, and these should form the basis for regular and in-depth discussions of future defense plans. Finally, transparency should be expanded by a commitment to share national intelligence information, using the precedent of what is now occurring within the UN Special Commission on Iraq. Past controls can be relaxed, now that the system of opposing blocs in Europe has disappeared.

The current regime of CSBMs was designed to ensure that the practices of military exercises and operations were not placed in jeopardy. Since military requirements have changed dramatically, this regime needs revision. To capture what could be considered serious military activities by the smaller countries in Europe, the thresholds for notification and observation of military activities should be lowered substantially, e.g., down to echelons at the regiment and brigade level, or numerical levels of around 3,000 troops.

For fear of constraining military exercises and mobilization, past treaties contain no genuine stabilizing measures beyond provisions in the CFE Treaty for notification of the removal of equipment from monitored storage sites. New measures need to be put in place to help ensure that the current situation is not destabilized by the activities of military forces anywhere in Europe. These should include requirements for notification in advance of the call-up of reservists and for the movement of equipment exceeding certain low levels. More militarily significant constraints need to be placed on the actual activities of military forces that nations would find necessary for their reconstitution. The specific details require negotiation, but limits could be placed on the size and frequency of military exercises, the number of troops simultaneously out of garrisons, the time period in which such activities could be held, the radius of movement, and movements toward border areas.

The CSBM regime currently does not cover alert exercises, those that are called with little or no advance notice. Notification is required only upon their initiation, and this loophole should be closed, although not necessarily for forces being readied for peacekeeping or peacemaking actions on short notice. With nations no longer worried about preparing for short-warning attacks, such exercises are not as important as they once were. Limits need to be placed on the number of permitted alert exercises, on their duration, and on the distance that forces could move out of garrison during such an exercise. Further steps should also be taken to keep readiness low: by constraining the percentage of equipment in active units and by placing real limits on the number of active-duty personnel. Other readiness measures should include limits on the size, location, and duration of mobilization activities.

Finally, arms control can help underpin and promote steps toward further economic and political integration within Europe. Cooperation and collective action directed toward regulating the production of military equipment would be one step, and another would be reducing arms sales. In addition to agreements under the auspices of the UN, the CSCE should look for ways to limit the transfer of sophisticated military weapons, including those of the United States, and perhaps even new technologies.

- **Arms control should provide means for managing the demilitarization of interstate relations in Europe and, over time, of helping foster a community of interest throughout Europe such that disputes are resolved peacefully.**

The levels of military capabilities in Europe mandated by the CFE Treaty reflect neither the current planning of governments nor the changes that have occurred in the security environment. Even after its full implementation, the signatories will be permitted to deploy some 158,000 pieces of major conventional equipment. All European states claim rhetorically that Europe needs to be further demilitarized; indeed, most are moving to reduce their military forces and place greater reliance on reserves and mobilization. But unilateral actions can be reversed. Smaller countries may still feel threatened. Residual force structures may accentuate offensive rather than defensive capabilities.

An initial arms control measure would be to gain further reductions in the forces of the major military powers in Europe. One simple way would be to lower significantly the sufficiency percentage in the CFE Treaty. Under that provision, any one country cannot possess within its area of application more than a certain percentage (33 percent) of treaty-limited equipment. Even without changing the overall ceilings on conventional forces, a sufficiency percentage of 5 percent of the total would ensure that no one country deployed more than 2,000 tanks, 3,000 armored vehicles, 2,000 artillery pieces, 680 combat aircraft, or 200 helicopters. With such a change, the equipment permitted the forces of Russia, Ukraine, Germany, and Turkey, as well as the United States, would be significantly lower. (See Table 3.)

Stability in Europe is threatened by what is happening within various countries as a result of the economic and political dislocations.

Military forces in all the countries of the former Soviet empire are facing special hardships. Their fate deserves attention, beyond gaining reductions in their size and capabilities. The concept of arms control needs to be expanded to include activities focused on integrating national militaries into their own state's civil democratic societies. Information should be shared among states as to the appropriate roles and activities of military forces. Building homes for retiring armies may be a more effective way of reducing forces than imposing ceilings. Beyond the aid provided by Germany for constructing homes for returning Soviet military forces, financial assistance will be required to help former soldiers make the transition to civilian life. Those engaged in the past for building the military machines in these countries need to be employed in their dismantlement. NATO's North Atlantic Cooperation Council has undertaken some preliminary civil-military efforts, but so far governments have not been willing to offer sufficient aid.

Finally, arms control provides the means of channeling the impending reductions in conventional military forces in Europe into force postures that are restructured to emphasize less threatening military capabilities and are reduced to minimum levels. The first task is to develop a common understanding of what a defensive restructuring of the military forces in Europe would require, consistent with maintaining security. Some attributes of a defensive military posture are clear: few immediately ready forces capable of projecting power beyond their national territory; greater dependence upon mobilization of reserves; highly survivable command and control systems; and stationary, largely immobile, defenses. The military objectives of such a defensive posture would be to defeat aggression by restoring prewar borders. All the arms control measures previously recommended promote this goal of a defensive restructuring.

Problems arise because individual weapon systems cannot easily be categorized as either offensive or defensive, stabilizing or destabilizing. But some systems seem to help the defender, e.g., anti-tank weapons and combat air-support aircraft, while others appear to give an advantage to the attacker, e.g., tanks, long-range fighter-bomber aircraft, mobile air defenses, and long-range missiles. Indeed, the CFE Treaty sought limits on the most threatening conventional weapon systems. One further step would be to reduce surface-to-surface missiles, a weapon system omitted from the limits in the CFE Treaty because of its nuclear role. That role has now disappeared.

The CSCE discussions on military doctrine offer a venue for discovering whether a consensus can be established over what would constitute a defensive military posture and what weapon systems should be given priorities in reductions. The overall goal would be to produce guidelines for the redesign of military doctrine, force postures, and operations for a Europe in which cooperation, not conflict, is the norm.

But agreement on what constitutes a defensive military posture will not be sufficient. A country's armed forces may be needed for military roles beyond the defense of national territory. This was the case in UN-sponsored actions to defeat the Iraqi aggression in the Gulf War. Such military operations will require more offensively structured forces and military equipment.

Depending upon how political developments proceed in Europe, arms control could provide a solution to this dilemma over the longer term. For the purpose of maintaining peace internationally, nations could place their offensive and power-projection military forces under the control of international institutions. These could be regional, or they could be drawn from around the globe under the UN. The goal would be to provide sufficient offensive firepower collectively in the defense of international peace and security. Individual countries in Europe could even specialize in certain offensive tasks, e.g., airlift and sealift, fighter aircraft, or mobile logistics. The remaining national forces within countries that retain selected force-projection capabilities would be restructured defensively.

- **Arms control should contribute to a significant reduction in the role of nuclear weapons and strengthen the global nuclear nonproliferation regime.**

An impressive number of steps have been taken to reduce nuclear weapons in Europe and to enhance the nuclear nonproliferation regime. All land-based tactical nuclear weapons will be eliminated. Germany, at the time of its unification, reaffirmed its commitment to foregoing the acquisition of nuclear, chemical, and biological weapons. The republics of the former Soviet Union have all promised to join the Non-Proliferation Treaty, with only Russia as a nuclear weapon state. Nuclear weapons are being brought under Russian central control. The International Atomic Energy Agency (IAEA) inspection regime of the NPT has been bolstered by agreement to activate its authority to conduct challenge inspections of suspected sites for nuclear weapons and their production.

Now the resources and technical expertise need to be found to assist in the disarming and destruction of the nuclear weapons systems, which the governments of the former republics of the Soviet Union have promised. It would also be useful for arrangements to be made for the joint or international monitoring of the destruction of those weapons to be reduced unilaterally by the Russians and Americans.

The problem is that the dangers of nuclear weapons do not disappear with these steps. Preventing the proliferation of nuclear weapons in Europe needs further attention, and arms control has an important role to play. The NPT provides the essential framework, and its renewal in 1995 is key. The CSCE countries could bolster the global NPT regime by extending IAEA challenge inspections within Europe to include nuclear facilities and military bases. They should implement the German proposal for an international convention to prevent the export of nuclear-weapon technology to third countries and back this with sanctions against any would-be nuclear power. Intelligence on nuclear proliferation issues should be more broadly shared among all governments in Europe, and they should begin contingency planning to intercept potential transfers of nuclear weapons and technologies.

But this still may not be enough to remove the dangers of nuclear weapons in Europe. Countries may turn to nuclear weapons to protect their security in the midst of the rising turmoil. The various arms control measures recommended for conventional forces should help, but moving to nonthreatening defensive conventional force postures throughout Europe will take time.

The response in the past of states possessing nuclear weapons has been to extend security guarantees to the nonnuclear states, as the United States has done for western Europeans. The problem with this response is that neither the Americans nor those in Western Europe seem willing to extend security guarantees to other countries in Europe. Even the need for American security guarantees for Western Europe is being questioned in light of the disappearance of the Soviet threat. Another response is required.

The existing nuclear-weapon states need to reduce the incentives of others to acquire nuclear weapons. One way to do this might be to lead by example—by reducing significantly their own reliance on nuclear weapons as the means for assuring their security. The nuclear powers in Europe would undertake to negotiate the elimination of all nonstrategic nuclear weapons, including all such air-delivered weapons. All nuclear powers, including Great Britain and France, would begin negotiations for further reductions in their nuclear forces, beyond those currently planned, with the goal of moving collectively to minimum deterrent postures. Those postures would be defined anew in light of the changed global security environment. To demonstrate their commitment to the global nonproliferation regime, the nuclear weapon states would also undertake to conclude a Comprehensive Test Ban in advance of the 1995 NPT review conference.

While the existence of nuclear weapons contributes to deterring any use of military forces, their central purpose in the future would be to deter the use of such weapons by others. Such a nuclear strategy is consistent with what has occurred politically and militarily in Europe. American nuclear weapons are no longer required to deter a major nuclear or conventional war. Americans will not lose their interest in helping keep the peace in Europe, if all their nuclear weapons are removed. On balance, the small risks that might arise as a result of these changes in the nuclear postures of Britain, France, and the United States are worth the potential gains in preventing the proliferation of nuclear weapons in Europe.

The possibility that the nuclear nonproliferation strategy may fail among the republics of the former Soviet Union and the countries on the southern and southeastern periphery of Europe has led to a renewed interest in limited missile defenses. Arms control offers an alternative response to this potential threat. In addition to measures to reinforce the NPT, limits could be placed on the number of long-range missiles, as well as on their sales. The Missile Technology Control Regime is a first step in seeking to restrict the spread of advanced technologies that could be used to deliver nuclear and chemical weapons. But if limited defenses seem necessary, arms control should still play a role. Rather than simply abandoning the Antiballistic Missile (ABM) Treaty, those countries interested in deploying limited missile defense should join a renegotiated ABM Treaty. By ensuring that any deployments are regulated, such a treaty would reduce the potential for instabilities.

At present, political cooperation appears to be winning out in the new Europe. But peace should not be left to chance. The potential for conflicts still remains; as long as there are armaments, security in Europe will have a military dimension. Arms control, therefore, has a continuing role to play. But arms control measures need to serve a broader goal: to help create a Europe in which not only nuclear weapons but also military forces in general have lost their value as arbiters of conflicts of interests among states. Europe needs to become a society in which potential disputes are resolved peacefully and where security is assured collectively.